5 REASONS
GOD WANTS YOU TO
PROSPER

The Believer's Pathway to a Biblical Mindset of
Wealth, Prosperity, and Abundance

REVISED & UPDATED ANNIVERSARY EDITION

SEBASTIEN RICHARD

5 Reasons God Wants You to Prosper: The Believer's Pathway to a Biblical Mindset of Wealth, Prosperity, and Abundance – Revised & Updated Anniversary Edition

Cover design by: Sebastien Richard

Interior formatting by: https://christianbookeditor.uk/

ISBN: 978-1-997555-00-1

THRIVING ❖ PURPOSE

http://www.thrivingonpurpose.com/

Dedicated to My Father in Heaven

*May this literary offering
bring glory and honor
to Your holy name.*

*May all who read it
be reassured and reconciled,
knowing that You are truly good,
that Your love endures forever,
that You delight in their prosperity,
and that Your faithfulness continues
through all generations.*

TABLE OF CONTENTS

PREFACE

What you are about to read in the following pages took me far too long to understand.

It also required a great deal of suffering and hardship to fully grasp.

You see, I grew up poor in Montreal, Quebec (Canada). For most of my youth, my parents were on welfare, so I became well acquainted with poverty.

My dad taught me that rich people were almost always wicked and "out to get you." As for my mom, she constantly reminded me that money doesn't buy happiness and that we were destined to get the short end of the stick. Unfortunately, she was right—we did get the short end of the stick.

As a result, I grew up believing that having money was something to be avoided. As crazy as that sounds, my deeply entrenched belief system told me that riches were evil and worldly, while poverty was virtuous and spiritual.

To make matters worse, in my Christian walk, I was taught—and believed—that riches would keep me from the Kingdom of Heaven. This was largely due to a misinterpretation of Jesus' teaching and its context. Sad, isn't it?

Even sadder is how much pain this belief system (B.S.) brought me:

- It kept me broke, in debt, and struggling financially for years.

- It almost destroyed my marriage to Elisabeth—on many occasions.

- It distorted my perception of God and damaged my relationship with Him.

- It made me a poor provider for my family.

But, thankfully, *"this poor man called, and the Lord heard him; He saved him out of all his troubles"* (Psalm 34:6, NIV).

By His mercy, the Lord also taught me right thinking about biblical prosperity through many great teachers and books. The learning curve was steep, and it took years, but in the end, I came out wiser and victorious! *Glory to God!*

In hindsight, the one good thing that came from growing up poor was that it pushed me to seek answers that otherwise would have eluded me. And in this book, I will openly share many of those answers concerning God's will for your prosperity.

So, dear friend, my goal in writing this book is to spare you—if possible—the trouble I endured and to lead you into right believing about God, prosperity, and what the Bible truly teaches about wealth.

I wrote this with urgency, conviction, compassion, and transparency. Now more than ever, I believe we are living in a time when believers *must* prosper in order to spread the gospel of the Kingdom throughout the entire world—for the time is at hand!

With every fiber of my being, I believe this book will accomplish its purpose: to guide believers into a victorious and prosperous mindset that will enable them to take back territory from the Enemy.

I pray it will profoundly bless you and empower you to prosper—God's way.

Sincerely,

Sebastien Richard,

Author & Bible Teacher

*"Blessed is the man
who walks not in the counsel of the wicked,
nor stands in the way of sinners,
nor sits in the seat of scoffers;
but his delight is in the law of the Lord,
and on his law he meditates day and night.*

*He is like a tree planted by streams of water
that yields its fruit in its season,
and its leaf does not wither.
In all that he does, he prospers."*

~Psalm 1:1-3 (ESV)

INTRODUCTION

Back in 1995, at 21 years old, I attended a powerful and convincing business presentation that led me to proudly enroll as an independent business owner with Amway, a well-known and successful network marketing company.

However, at the time, I was also a deeply religious young man—and I don't mean that in a good way.

You see, I had convinced myself that Jesus wanted me to be poor because poverty kept me humble and supposedly glorified Him.

I believed that no rich man could enter the Kingdom of Heaven and that I was somehow better than all those "filthy rich" people. This perverse and self-righteous mindset gave me a poor self-image and an even poorer bank account. I'll share more on that later.

Without realizing it, I had much in common with the Pharisee in Jesus' parable of the Pharisee and the Tax Collector (Luke 18:9-14):

"To some who were confident of their own righteousness and looked down on everyone else,

Jesus told this parable: 'Two men went up to the temple to pray, one a Pharisee and the other a tax collector. The Pharisee stood by himself and prayed: "God, I thank you that I am not like other people— robbers, evildoers, adulterers—or even like this tax collector. I fast twice a week and give a tenth of all I get."

But the tax collector stood at a distance. He would not even look up to heaven, but beat his breast and said, "God, have mercy on me, a sinner."

I tell you that this man, rather than the other, went home justified before God. For all those who exalt themselves will be humbled, and those who humble themselves will be exalted."'

It was with that Pharisaic mindset that I attended a massive Amway conference in Toronto. And I was *horrified* by what I saw:

- People going on stage and, in my eyes, *boasting* about their financial success.
- Attendees talking only about the trips they took, the cars they bought, and the mortgages they paid off.
- Speakers quoting the Bible while discussing wealth and financial freedom (*how dare they!*).

- People exchanging personal development books like highly coveted treasures.
- Entrepreneurs boldly declaring that God wanted them to be successful.

I remember feeling deeply offended. *How dare these worldly Christians and pagans use the Word of God to justify becoming rich!?*

In my self-righteous indignation, I saw myself as Jesus in the temple, surrounded by greedy moneychangers.

So, when I got back from the conference, I made it my mission to quit this "filthy" Amway business—because, in my mind, it was ungodly.

Walking away felt like I had just escaped the *Beast system* of the great prostitute from Revelation. *I kid you not!*

Fast Forward to Today...

And here I am, having written the very book you are now reading: *5 Reasons God Wants YOU to Prosper.*

Talk about a 180-degree turn!

So, what changed?

What made me go from believing *"God wants you to be poor because the love of money is the root of all evil"* to *"God wants you to succeed and prosper"*?

Well, have you ever heard the saying, *"When you change the way you look at things, the things you look at change"*?

That's exactly what happened to me.

I won't go into all the details of my financial learning journey here, but suffice it to say that I began looking at God's Word differently. And as I did, it started changing—not just in how I understood it, but in how it transformed me.

But this process didn't happen overnight. It took years for my thinking to shift into what it is today.

Let's just say God has been very patient with me—and He still is.

Money Is on God's Mind

How we handle our money is one of the clearest indicators of the condition of our soul and heart. It's also a topic God emphasized heavily in Scripture. Consider this:

- The Bible contains over 500 references to prayer and nearly 500 references to faith—but over 2,000 references to money and possessions!

- Out of 38 parables that Jesus told in the Gospels, 16 deal with money and how we handle it.

- Jesus spoke more about money and possessions than He did about heaven and hell *combined*.

- One out of every ten verses in the Gospels—288 verses in total—deals with money or possessions.

So, clearly, this is a topic God wants us to understand.

What you're about to read in this book is the result of years of study, mind-shifting, and seeking God in prayer about finances, success, and His will for His people.

My Hope for You

I hope this short book will challenge you to change the way you look at things—so that the things you look at may change. In all honesty, that's the only way to grow.

Before you dive in, let me give you a heads-up: Some of the concepts, philosophies, and ideas in this book may go against everything you currently believe—just as they did for me at first. Some of it may be new to you, even shocking. You might even find certain ideas offensive.

But I urge you—read to the very end. Don't make the same mistake I did. Don't reject this message in a knee-jerk reaction like I once did. Being open-minded to what I've written here could save you *years* of misery, struggle, and missing out on God's best for your life. Hey, it might even save your marriage. Trust me on this one.

Aristotle once said, *"It is the mark of an educated mind to be able to entertain a thought without accepting it."*

In other words, *be teachable*. Be open-minded. Be curious.

With that said, let's dig in.

I know some of you are probably thinking, *"I don't believe it's God's will for me to be rich. That goes against everything I know about Him."*

And you know what? I'm willing to concede that point—at least for now. Maybe you're right. Maybe

God *doesn't* want you to be rich (and we'll define *rich* later).

But here's something you can take to the bank (*pun intended*):

It Is NOT God's Will for You to Be Poor

Whether God wants you to be comfortable, well-off, rich, or super-wealthy—that's between you and Him. But one thing I *do* know for certain is that God has no desire or purpose for you to be poor.

You might ask, *"How do you know?"*

Simple. I've read the Bible. I've studied it carefully for decades. I've also studied the lives and teachings of wealthy believers. More importantly, I *know* my Heavenly Father. I know His heart, His will, and His goodness. I've experienced His provision and blessings time and time again over the course of my 37-year walk with Him.

These are the primary reasons I'm convinced that God doesn't *want* or *need* you to be poor.

Now, am I saying it's a sin to be poor, to struggle financially, or to be in debt? Of course not. I've been there, and God didn't hold it against me.

Can God still use you if you're poor? Absolutely.

For every Job, there is a John the Baptist. And for every Abraham or Solomon, there were imprisoned, suffering, and struggling apostles who had "no gold or silver" (Acts 3:6).

Even as you read this, there are believers in other countries being persecuted, imprisoned, and even killed for their faith. Did God use them? Certainly. Did they have money? Probably not much.

So, let's be clear—God *can* and *does* use believers who are poor, sometimes in mighty ways.

But here's the real question: *Does He use them because they are poor, as some believe? Or does He use them despite their poverty?*

That distinction matters.

As someone once said, *"Poverty is no disgrace, but that's about all that can be said in its favor."*

Here's the thing: God can use people just the same—*and even more so*—if they have money.

Consider this: Job has an entire book named after him, Solomon authored numerous books

(Ecclesiastes 12:12), yet John the Baptist—who surely had much to say—left behind no written work.

In the Old Testament, God told His people:

"There should be no poor among you, for the LORD your God will greatly bless you in the land He is giving you as a special possession." ~Deuteronomy 15:4 (NLT)

When Moses penned these words, it was clear that God wanted His people to have provision—to have more than enough. He planned for it. He expected it.

And today, we live under the New Covenant—*a better covenant* (Hebrews 8:6-12).

If God prepared provision for His people under the Old Covenant, wouldn't He do even *more* under the New?

Of course, He would.

Now, do you believe that?

Even more importantly... do you believe it *for yourself*?

Whatever your current stance on this issue, I hope you'll stick around as we explore the five reasons God *wants* to prosper you—not harm you (*Jeremiah 29:11*). He *does* have plans to give you a future and a hope.

It's my conviction, dear friend, that you will be blessed as you continue reading this book.

CHAPTER 1

God Wants You Fully Alive

The first thing believers must establish regarding God and their finances is this: God, your Father and King, is the God of the living.

This foundational truth is absolutely critical as you begin your biblical schooling on prosperity.

At this point, you might be wondering, *"What does this have to do with the price of tea in China?"* Or perhaps, *"What does this have to do with why God wants me to prosper?"*

That's a fair question—one that deserves a good answer. So, bear with me.

When debating the Sadducees on the resurrection, Jesus told them they were gravely mistaken. He then ended His explanation with a powerful statement:

"He is not the God of the dead, but of the living, for to Him all are alive." ~Luke 20:38

Jesus also declared in John 10:10:

"I have come that they may have life, and have it to the full." (NIV)

The New Living Translation (NLT) phrases it this way:

"My purpose is to give them a rich and satisfying life."

From the very beginning, as the book of Genesis attests, God is the author of life. And to understand even a fraction of what it means that He is the *God of the living*, we must understand the nature of this thing called life—which He created.

Growth: The Evidence of Life

John Henry Newman once said, *"Growth is the only evidence of life."*

All living things grow and expand—it is their natural inclination. Consider:

- Cells grow and multiply.
- Blades of grass grow.
- Plants and trees grow from a tiny seed.

- Animals grow from a microscopic egg or fetus.
- Human beings grow.

Unlike the rest of creation, however, human beings are unique. They are made in the image of God (Genesis 1:27). While our bodies grow automatically through physical nourishment, our minds and souls grow intentionally. Humanity's potential for growth is limitless, and we are driven by an inner desire to expand—whether in knowledge, skills, wealth, influence, or impact.

Make no mistake: God placed this drive for growth within us.

If you ask most people what they want in life, their answer will likely be, *"More than I have now."* That desire is not greed—it is the built-in programming of life-expansion that God hardwired into mankind.

The Image of God in Your Desire for Growth

Your desire to grow and expand is a reflection of God's nature.

God, when He created the universe, was expressing Himself—expanding His presence through creation. And since you are made in His image, you naturally desire to grow, create, and expand as well.

Wallace D. Wattles, in *The Science of Getting Rich*, described this human desire for more as follows:

"The desire for riches is simply the capacity for larger life seeking fulfillment... That which makes you want more money is the same as that which makes the plant grow; it is life seeking fuller expression... It is the desire of God that you should get rich. He wants you to get rich because He can express Himself better through you if you have plenty of things to use in giving Him expression. He can live more in you if you have unlimited command of the means of life."

I understand—these words may rub you the wrong way. They used to bother me too. But I encourage you to keep reading. By the time you finish this book, you will see why they are true.

God's Desire for You to Reach Your Full Potential

God, the Author of life, has placed within you a deep-seated drive to grow—just as He placed within an acorn the capacity to become a mighty oak tree.

The early Church Father Irenaeus once said: *"The glory of God is man fully alive."*

A human being who seeks to grow, expand, and reach his full potential glorifies God. That is *man fully alive.*

So, let me ask you some important questions:

- How much should you grow?
- How much success should you aim for?
- How much money should you make?

The answer to all three is simple: As much as you possibly can.

Why? Because God desires nothing less for you than your full potential.

John Wesley, in his famous sermon *The Use of Money*, put it this way: *"Earn all you can, give all you can, save all you can."*

Jim Rohn, a renowned speaker on business success, said:

"How much should you earn? As much as you possibly can. It doesn't matter whether you earn $10,000 a year or $1,000,000 a year. As long as you've done the best you can, God will take care of the rest."

The Law of Potential in God's Creation

Everything in God's creation grows as much as it possibly can:

- Grass grows as tall as it possibly can.
- A tree grows as high as it possibly can.
- Every creature in nature strives to reach its full potential.

Yet, among all creation, only human beings hold themselves back—crippled by self-limiting beliefs and negative thoughts. God forbid!

The God of life and growth wants you to be like the tree described in Psalm 1:3:

"He will be like a tree firmly planted by streams of water, which yields its fruit in its season and its leaf does not wither; and in whatever he does, he prospers." (NASB)

God doesn't want you to wither—He wants you to *thrive*.

So, the question is: Will you embrace the fullness of life and growth that God desires for you?

CHAPTER 2

God Wants to Establish His Covenant

The Bible tells us plainly in Deuteronomy 8:18:

"You shall remember the Lord your God, for it is He who gives you power to get wealth, that He may establish His covenant which He swore to your fathers, as it is this day." (NKJV)

Other translations render it as follows:

- NIV: *"The ability to produce wealth."*
- NASB: *"The power to make wealth."*
- The Message: *"Your God gave you the strength to produce all this wealth."*

This powerful passage of Scripture presents some fascinating truths.

1. God Desires Our Prosperity

Why would God give man the ability, power, or strength to produce wealth unless He *wanted* man to be wealthy? This verse confirms that prosperity is part of God's desire for His people.

2. Wealth Creation and Entrepreneurship

There is a foundational principle within this ability to create wealth that aligns with business ownership. I firmly believe that believers should, as much as possible, strive to become entrepreneurs.

Our ability to create wealth is greatly *stunted* when we merely offer our skills as employees. Conversely, when we step into business ownership, our ability to generate wealth is greatly *multiplied.*

3. God's Purpose: Establishing His Covenant

The key word in Deuteronomy 8:18 is *"establish."*

Merriam-Webster defines *establish* as:

1. *To institute (something, such as a law) permanently by enactment or agreement.*

2. *(a) To make firm or stable.*
   (b) To introduce and cause to grow and multiply.

God's covenant in the Old Testament was ultimately meant to bring forth the Kingdom of God, which Christ solidified through His work on the cross.

From the moment Jesus arrived, everything became about the Kingdom. Establishing His covenant today means spreading *"The Good News of the Kingdom"* (Luke 4:43). And one of the ways God enables us to do this is by giving us the ability to create wealth.

Believers in Business

Josh Tolley, in his excellent book *Evangelpreneur: How Biblical Free Enterprise Can Empower Your Faith, Family, and Freedom*, stresses the importance of believers engaging in business. He also clarifies the different types of workers found in Scripture.

Four Categories of Workers in the Bible:

1. Slaves

Slaves were considered property and had little to no rights. In biblical times, people became slaves through war or debt. However, civil law required owners to release slaves after six years. While unlawful, human trafficking did occur, as seen in Joseph's story (Genesis 37).

2. Laborers (Self-Employed Contractors)

Laborers were independent workers who negotiated wages for specific jobs. For example, a farmer might hire a laborer to harvest crops. Once the job was completed, the laborer was paid and free to move on. Their success depended on their skills and business sense.

A biblical example of laborers is found in Matthew 20:1-16, in the parable of the workers in the vineyard.

3. Masters (Entrepreneurs)

A *master* was an entrepreneur who, with God's blessing, expanded his business and influence. Examples include Abraham, Isaac, Jacob, and Job— all prosperous men of faith. Today, masters are equivalent to successful entrepreneurs.

4. Servants (Employees)

Servants had more freedom than slaves and received wages, but their lives were still largely controlled by their masters. They had set hours, limited earning potential, and minimal upward mobility. Servants typically wore clothing that represented their master—similar to today's uniforms and name tags.

Josh Tolley explains:

"If we were to be honest, most of us would acknowledge we are servants. We are not slaves, not laborers, and certainly not masters. The sad thing is, unlike in biblical times where servants became servants out of desperation, today we enter a similar arrangement voluntarily—and even encourage our children to do the same."

The Limitation of Employment

Let's be clear: God cannot fully establish His covenant through us if we remain employees for 25-30 years.

Now, is there honor in honest work? Absolutely. Am I condemning employment? Not at all.

I, myself, worked for Canada Post for 18 years as a mail carrier and mail sorter. That was my job. But the reality is that a *job* is not the way to use our "power to get wealth."

Remember what *job* stands for:

- **J**ust **O**ver **B**roke
- **J**ust **O**beying **B**osses

With set hours, limited vacation, and a salary ceiling, a job is simply a pair of golden handcuffs.

As Jim Rohn wisely said:

"If you don't design your own life plan, chances are you'll fall into someone else's plan. And guess what they have planned for you? Not much."

Your Dreams: God-Given Clues to Your Purpose

In the movie *Up in the Air* (2009), starring George Clooney, there's a powerful scene where a long-time employee, Bob, is being laid off. Clooney's character, Ryan Bingham, tells him:

"Kids admire those who follow their dreams. That's why they look up to professional athletes."

Then he asks: *"How much did they first pay you to give up on your dreams?"*

Bob sheepishly answers: *$27,000 a year.*

Ryan replies: *"You have an opportunity here, Bob. This is a rebirth. If not for you, then do it for your children."*

The truth is, many of us settled—trading our dreams for a steady paycheck. We were told pursuing dreams was irresponsible, impractical, and childish. We believed the lie that following our God-given desires would lead to poverty.

But what if the dreams in your heart are actually divine clues to your purpose, success, and ability to create wealth?

God has "plans to prosper you and not to harm you" (Jeremiah 29:11). He wants to establish His covenant through you—not against you. That's why He gives you both the ability to create wealth and the dreams to pursue it.

Your dreams are God's seeds of greatness within you. When those seeds sprout, you step into your purpose, discover your ability to create wealth, and glorify God in the process.

Your Ability, His Covenant, and His Kingdom

Your ability to create wealth serves two divine purposes:

1. **To Fulfill Your Purpose**

    - God aligns our desires and dreams with our unique Kingdom mandate. He has plans to prosper us, but we must actively seek His will.

2. **To Establish His Covenant**

- The New Covenant is about expanding His Kingdom—which requires resources. God knows you need money to make a lasting impact!

Even Jesus had financial resources during His ministry. Luke 8:1-3 tells us that faithful followers provided for Him "from their substance." If Jesus understood that funding was necessary for Kingdom expansion, shouldn't we?

As Al Capone once said (paraphrased):

"You can get much farther with the gospel and money than with the gospel alone."

Consider Billy Graham—one of the greatest evangelists of our time. His impact required magazines, TV, stadiums, and employees, and so much more—all of which required money. What was his estimated net worth when he passed? $25 million.

Billy Graham understood the ability to create wealth—and used it to establish God's covenant and expand the Kingdom.

So should we.

CHAPTER 3

God Delights in Your Prosperity

P icture This...

If I were to ask a gathering of Evangelicals the question:

"What does God delight in?"

It's easy to imagine the responses:

- He delights in our obedience.
- He delights in our faith.
- He delights in our praise.
- He delights in our knowledge of His Word.

These are all biblically sound answers.

But one response that likely wouldn't make it onto this *Family Feud*-style board is: He delights in our prosperity.

And yet, the Bible assures us that God does indeed delight in our prosperity.

In Psalm 35:27, we read:

"The Lord be magnified, who delights in the prosperity of His servant."

When I read this verse, it doesn't just reassure me— it fills me with joy! God actually wants us to succeed financially. He delights in our prosperity so much that Scripture tells us He even plans for it.

Consider Jeremiah 29:11:

"For I know the plans I have for you," declares the Lord, "plans to prosper you and not to harm you, plans to give you hope and a future."

Yet, despite these clear biblical affirmations, many believers struggle with this idea. Somehow, they find it difficult to accept that God both delights in and plans for our prosperity.

But why?

As parents, we naturally delight in the prosperity and success of our children. Why should God be any different? In fact, to paraphrase Scripture, we could say:

"If you then, though you are evil, delight in the prosperity of your children, how much more will your Father in heaven delight in yours?"

The Bible tells us that our own goodness is as *filthy rags* before Him (Isaiah 64:6), yet we presume that our love for our children is greater than His love for us?

Now, can you spell p-r-i-d-e?

Because pride and presumption are exactly what lead to such distorted views of God.

Why Does God Delight in Our Prosperity?

The answer is twofold:

1. He wants His covenant established (as we'll see later).
2. He loves us—plain and simple.

Here's something I've noticed about the most prosperous believers:

They never doubt His love.

They believe that because God loves them, He delights in their prosperity. And this is no coincidence.

By contrast, I've also observed that Christians who focus more on what I call negative scriptural truths—such as their own sinful nature, God's judgments, or His anger—tend to be less prosperous than those who focus on His love, power, grace, and blessings.

The math is simple:

Those who expect great things from God receive great things from God. Those who believe God delights in their prosperity are the ones who prosper the most.

A pastor once asked a thought-provoking question:

"We call ourselves believers, but what do we believe?"

So, let me ask you:

Do you believe that God delights in your prosperity? Do you believe that He truly wants to prosper you and not harm you? *(Jeremiah 29:11)*

Wealth: A Blessing or a Curse?

While researching for this book, I came across a sermon by a well-known evangelical pastor. In this clip, he passionately preached against wealth—no doubt as a reaction to the so-called prosperity gospel.

His anger was palpable. His eyes bulged, veins protruded from his forehead, and he spat out his words as he declared. screaming:

"Wealth is almost always a curse!"

He used familiar Scriptures to make his point:

- *"The love of money is the root of all evil"* (1 Timothy 6:10).

- *"It is easier for a camel to go through the eye of a needle than for a rich man to enter the kingdom of heaven"* (Matthew 19:24).

These verses are frequently cited to condemn wealth and, at times, even to glorify poverty.

Ironically, however, these same pastors will often ask their congregation to give generously to their church or ministry.

Now, don't get me wrong—giving is important. I wholeheartedly believe in generosity, tithing (the right way), and supporting the work of God.

But let's be honest.

It's hypocritical for pastors to preach against prosperity while depending on the wealth of their congregation to keep their ministries afloat.

How Much Is Too Much?

So, how can you and I keep a healthy view of wealth? How can we enjoy God's financial blessing while avoiding it becoming a stumbling block for us?

I have often been asked: *How much money is too much money?* At what point does money stop being a blessing and become a problem—perhaps even a curse?

The answer is fairly simple.

Have you ever heard the expression, *"Every man has his price"*?

This means that whatever amount begins to steer you into a love relationship with money is too much for you. The amount that would make you compromise your integrity or devotion to God is too much wealth. That's it. Simple, isn't it?

So, whatever amount would make you shift from serving God to serving Mammon is your threshold. And this amount varies from person to person. For one person, $50,000 a year is their price because they get greedy easily. For another, it might be $50 million.

Whatever the case may be, if you fear becoming ensnared by the love of money, you can pray along with Agur:

"Give me neither poverty nor riches; feed me with the food that is needful for me, lest I be full and deny you and say, 'Who is the Lord?' or lest I be poor and steal and profane the name of my God." ~Proverbs 30:8-9, ESV

But keep in mind that if you pray this way, you may be limiting your full potential and depriving your Father in heaven of delighting in your prosperity.

What Is Biblical Prosperity?

At this point, it may be necessary for me to define my understanding of biblical prosperity.

I don't believe (or endorse, or teach) that God wants every single one of us to be multi-millionaires or billionaires. He may want some of us to become very wealthy for varying reasons and purposes, but this is by no means a blueprint for all believers.

Just as in nature not all oak trees reach the same height, not everyone has the capacity to build vast fortunes. Besides, not everyone can handle millions of dollars adequately and in a God-honoring way. As the parable of the talents points out, He gave "to each according to his own ability."

While the prosperity God wants for you and me is not necessarily excessive, it is nonetheless—and most definitely—more than enough. And, not meaning to offend, it is more than most of my readers enjoy at this point.

2 Corinthians 9:8 (CEB) says:

"God has the power to provide you with more than enough of every kind of grace. That way, you will have everything you need always and in everything to provide more than enough for every kind of good work."

More than enough means God delights in the following:

- You having no financial debt.

- You having more than enough to pay all your bills.

- You having more than enough money to fulfill every Kingdom assignment He has for you.

- You having more than enough left over to help others fulfill theirs.

This, dear friend, is what our loving God and Father delights in! This is biblical prosperity.

CHAPTER 4

God Wants You to be Good and Generous

Before I became a Kingdom entrepreneur, there was a particular verse that always stung me whenever I read it. Proverbs 13:22 says, *"A good man leaves an inheritance to his children's children, but the sinner's wealth is laid up for the righteous."*

Why did it sting? Because every time I read it, I knew I didn't measure up to the biblical definition of a good man. My debts, combined with my $50,000-a-year salary, weren't enough to provide for my children's children (my future grandchildren) and therefore didn't qualify me as a good man. It wasn't even enough to provide adequately for my children, let alone my grandchildren! As a result, this verse often left me feeling downcast.

Nevertheless, I knew that God wanted me to be a good man. I understood that providing for my children and grandchildren was part of His will for me.

With this firm belief, I began searching for ways to improve—to become the kind of good man described in Proverbs 13:22. And unless you become a doctor, lawyer, or CEO, the best way to do this is to become an entrepreneur—or, as the Bible calls them, a *Master*.

Why Does God Call the Prosperous Man a Good Man?

The reason God refers to the prosperous man as a *good man* is threefold:

1. A Good Man Takes Care of His Family

Paul echoes Proverbs 13:22 in 1 Timothy 5:8:

"If someone does not provide for his own, especially his own family, he has denied the faith and is worse than an unbeliever."

Most of us were raised with the understanding that a good man provides for his family's needs. This is a biblical principle. In times past, men were taught to be providers.

The word *provide* comes from two Latin roots: *pro*, meaning "ahead," and *video*, meaning "to see." A good provider is someone who *sees ahead* and makes provision.

Living in Eastern Canada, I've seen this principle in action every winter. When a major snowstorm is forecasted, it's common for Canadians to rush to the nearest Walmart to gather provisions for at least 72 hours.

Why?

Because we see the necessity of preparing for the storm—we anticipate the challenge and make provision accordingly.

In the same way, a good man who is prosperous provides for his children's children by planning for their future. He ensures their security by looking ahead.

2. A Good Man Is a Good Steward of God's Resources

Many parallels can be drawn between the good man of Proverbs 13:22 and the *good and faithful servant* in the Parable of the Talents.

I believe Jesus had this very verse in mind when He taught that parable. The latter part of Proverbs 13:22

states, *"The sinner's wealth is laid up for the righteous."*

This aligns with the fate of the wicked servant in Matthew 25:28-30:

"Take the talent from him and give it to him who has the ten talents. For to everyone who has, more will be given, and he will have an abundance. But from the one who has not, even what he has will be taken away. And cast the worthless servant into the outer darkness. In that place, there will be weeping and gnashing of teeth."

Our Lord takes fruitfulness very seriously. Yet many believers mistakenly think God is only concerned with spiritual growth. That isn't true.

Righteousness isn't just about salvation and sanctification—it also involves being fruitful in every area of life, including finances.

Though often spiritualized, the Parable of the Talents is ultimately a lesson on stewardship and resource management. It underscores God's desire for us to *grow* what He has entrusted to us.

However, many Christians approach finances with the wrong mindset. They assume, *"If I spend less, I will have more."* Instead of focusing on creating wealth, they focus on cutting costs.

But that's the wrong approach. God desires financial expansion, not financial contraction.

Of course, frugality has its place, but it's not the foundation for good stewardship. God does not bless mismanagement, and viewing wealth solely through the lens of saving rather than growing is poor stewardship—it's akin to burying your talent in the ground.

Consider Job. While known for his righteousness, he was also an exceptional manager of resources. The same applies to Joseph. Many think Joseph was promoted because of his gift for interpreting dreams, but his rise to power came through his *administrative abilities.* His leadership skills brought him favor in Potiphar's house, in prison, and ultimately in Pharaoh's court.

3. A Good Man Cares for Others

God desires for His people to be generous. Proverbs 11:25 says, *"A generous person will prosper; whoever refreshes others will be refreshed."* Jesus reinforced this in Luke 6:38:

"Give, and it will be given to you. A good measure, pressed down, shaken together, and running over, will be poured into your lap. For with the measure you use, it will be measured to you."

There's an old story of a generous farmer who was asked why he gave so much yet remained prosperous.

"It's simple," he replied. *"I keep shoveling into God's bin, and He keeps shoveling into mine—but God has the bigger shovel."*

The truth is, the more we have, the more we can give. More resources allow us to help more people, support the poor, and advance the Kingdom.

2 Corinthians 9:8 makes this clear:

"And God is able to bless you abundantly, so that in all things at all times, having all that you need, you will abound in every good work."

Wealth enables us to *demonstrate* God's goodness through generosity.

Be a River, Not a Pond

Scripture warns against hoarding wealth for selfish gain. Ecclesiastes 5:13-14 states, *"I have seen a grievous evil under the sun: wealth hoarded to the harm of its owners."*

Jesus echoed this in Matthew 6:19-21:

"Do not store up for yourselves treasures on earth, where moths and vermin destroy, and where thieves break in and steal. But store up for yourselves treasures in heaven, where moths and vermin do not destroy, and where thieves do not break in and steal. For where your treasure is, there your heart will be also."

The Bible is clear: we are called to *create* wealth, but not *hoard* it.

As believers, we are meant to be *rivers of righteousness*, not *ponds of selfishness*. We are called to use our resources to be generous and bless others.

Jesus taught us to pray, *"Thy Kingdom come. Thy will be done on earth as it is in heaven."*

This prayer isn't just a call for God's influence—it's a declaration of our willingness to be vessels of His will. Kingdom citizens are called to use their resources to bring heaven's influence to earth.

Yet some believers act as if it's the other way around.

I know many who spend their time longing for heaven rather than impacting the earth. They pride themselves on being *grounded* in Christ, yet their heads are in the clouds—always thinking about *someday* in heaven while neglecting their earthly duty.

Oliver Wendell Holmes once said:

"Some people are so heavenly minded that they are no earthly good."

God's will isn't for us to passively wait for heaven—it's for us to actively bring His Kingdom to earth. That requires stewardship, generosity, and the wisdom to grow what He has entrusted to us. After all, it's what a good man (or woman) would do.

CHAPTER 5

God Wants His Kingdom to Expand

Jesus taught that the Kingdom of Heaven is meant to grow and expand. This principle is clearly illustrated in the parables of the mustard seed and the leaven:

"He put another parable before them, saying, 'The kingdom of heaven is like a grain of mustard seed that a man took and sowed in his field. It is the smallest of all seeds, but when it has grown, it is larger than all the garden plants and becomes a tree, so that the birds of the air come and make nests in its branches.'

He told them another parable. 'The kingdom of heaven is like leaven that a woman took and hid in three measures of flour until it was all leavened.'"
~Matthew 13:31-33 (ESV)

Clearly, the Kingdom's modus operandi is expansion—both within us (Luke 17:21) and throughout the world.

When we grow in spiritual maturity and contribute to the Kingdom's advancement, God entrusts us with more. As I mentioned earlier, God does not send growth where there is poor management. When we manage well, He gives us more responsibility—including financial prosperity.

The Father is best served when a righteous person has the means to influence and advance His Kingdom. Why? Because a righteous person will use those resources for God's purposes. In God's economy, that is precious.

Taking Back Territory

Since Jesus completed His mission of redeeming humanity, God has been working through believers—by the power of the Holy Spirit—to reclaim territory from the enemy.

Jesus declared:

"I will build my church, and the gates of hell shall not prevail against it. I will give you the keys of the kingdom of heaven, and whatever you bind on earth shall be bound in heaven, and whatever you loose

on earth shall be loosed in heaven." ~Matthew 16:18-19 (ESV)

Many interpret this passage to mean that the Church will stand firm against the enemy's attacks—but in reality, it means quite the opposite.

When Jesus said, *"The gates of hell shall not prevail,"* He wasn't saying the Church would merely defend itself against the enemy. He was saying that the strongholds of hell will not be able to withstand the advancing power of the Church. The Church is not on the defensive—*it is on the offensive.*

Imagine a medieval battle where soldiers lay siege to a fortress. One of the most effective tools in such an assault was the battering ram—a massive log wielded by several men to repeatedly strike a fortified gate until it broke under the relentless force.

This is the picture Jesus painted: the Church is not retreating—it is storming the gates of hell, reclaiming territory for the Kingdom of God.

This is the Church that Jesus came to establish—bold, strong, and, contrary to what many believe, designed for assault!

The Church was never meant to sit idly under the enemy's attacks. Instead, it was created to storm the gates of hell, reclaiming territory for the King and His Kingdom. The Kingdom of God is proactive, not reactive.

God's rule and influence have now been restored in the hearts and lives of those who serve Him. Every day, men and women advance His Kingdom by doing His will—taking back territory from the enemy. And yes, this includes engaging in business and acquiring wealth for His glory.

When you or I bring Kingdom influence into the marketplace—through a business or organization dedicated to serving the Most High—we are reclaiming territory from the enemy. This is even more evident when we reinvest our profits into the Kingdom by sowing financial seeds into Christian organizations. Through this, we advance His Kingdom's influence.

This is the mandate we are under until Jesus Christ returns to restore all things.

In the meantime, Jesus commanded us to assault the gates of hell and to *"occupy till I come"* (Luke 19:13). In the parable of the talents, the master (representing Christ) gives his servants this instruction before leaving: *"Occupy till I come."*

So, what does it mean to occupy *until He comes?*

Essentially, Jesus was telling us to remain actively engaged in expanding His Kingdom. The English Standard Version translates *"occupy till I come"* as *"engage in business until I come."* In other words: *Take care of my business, make it grow, and manage it well while I'm gone.* The parable of the talents, from which this phrase originates, directly relates to conducting business and increasing wealth. It teaches Kingdom expansion through financial stewardship.

Interestingly, *occupy* can also be understood in military terms. To *occupy* means to take control of a territory, especially by conquest or settlement. Synonyms include *capture, seize, take possession of, conquer, invade, overrun, take over, or colonize.*

Isn't that remarkable?

A steadfast believer who builds a business and succeeds financially will often use his resources to invest in the Kingdom. He sows financial seeds of righteousness and gains new ground for God. As the prayer of Jabez says in 1 Chronicles 4:10, *"Enlarge my territory."*

Think about it—who funds Christian schools, missionary organizations, youth ministries, camps, and new church buildings? It's Christians who have the financial means to do so. In other words, it's the Jobs, Abrahams, Davids, Solomons, and Josephs of today.

God uses successful and wealthy believers to take back territory from the enemy.

This is just one more reason why God wants YOU to succeed and prosper financially!

CONCLUSION

As we conclude this book, let's take a moment to review the five key reasons why God desires your prosperity:

1. **God wants you fully alive.** He is the God of the living, and the essence of life is growth.

2. **God wants to establish His covenant.**

3. **God delights in your prosperity** (because He is good).

4. **God wants you to be good and generous.** More wealth gives you more to give.

5. **God wants His Kingdom to expand, not regress.** And yes, money plays a role in making this happen.

Considering these biblical truths, we can be certain that God wants to prosper you—not just for your benefit, but for His as well.

Some may find this a bold claim, but it is undeniably true.

Every king benefits when his people thrive. A prosperous kingdom reflects well on its ruler. When a kingdom flourishes, its citizens perceive the king in a positive light.

The Legacy of the Prosperity Gospel

The so-called *prosperity gospel*—also known as *prosperity theology*—has become controversial in the eyes of many.

This is primarily due to two reasons:

1. **The actions of certain preachers.** Some have flaunted their wealth, attracting negative media attention. Others have fallen into the love of money, becoming greedy and corrupt, damaging the reputation of prosperity teachings.

2. **A misunderstanding of biblical prosperity.** Many believers have failed to properly discern truth from error. Yet, as Christians, we are called to *"test all things; hold fast what is good. Abstain from every form of evil"* (1 Thessalonians 5:21-22, NKJV).

A lack of discernment has led some to give large sums of money to untrustworthy individuals or ministries, only to see no return on their giving. Some were even deceived—conned by religion itself. This kind of disillusionment is hard to recover from.

Others have misunderstood the biblical principles of sowing and reaping, failing to see their financial harvest.

As a result, many Christians have rejected *all* teachings about prosperity—throwing out the baby with the bathwater.

Unfortunately, the media-fueled scandals of a few have caused many to develop an allergic reaction to the word *prosperity*—to their own detriment.

Some have taken such offense at certain preachers and their teachings that they instinctively reject anything resembling prosperity teaching.

They develop a knee-jerk reaction, perceiving all prosperity talk as inherently evil. In doing so, many unconsciously develop a hatred of money—believing this will safeguard them from *"the love of money"* (1 Timothy 6:10) and prevent them from being deceived again.

However, this reaction is unnecessary and, ultimately, self-destructive.

And yet, as we have seen, *God delights in our prosperity and success.*

Satan's Snare

So, what happens to Christians who reject prosperity?

They fall into something just as dangerous as the love of money—**a spirit of poverty.**

Yes, it's a trap.

The enemy prefers Christians who are broke, bound by debt, helpless, bitter, and fruitless. He rejoices when believers embrace a spirit of poverty because it serves his purpose: it weakens the impact of God's Kingdom.

But what is *a spirit of poverty*?

In an article for *Charisma Magazine* titled *7 Discernible Signs the Spirit of Poverty Is Attacking You,* author Dave Williams identifies seven key symptoms:

1. **A strong aversion to material wealth.** They condemn what they classify as *"materialism."*

2. **A mindset of resignation.** They comfort themselves with phrases like: *"Everyone has debts." "Others are struggling too." "This is just how life is."*

3. **Shame surrounding financial discussions.** The spirit of poverty convinces people that money matters are inappropriate to discuss, especially in church. It portrays lack as a virtue.

4. **Judgmental attitudes toward successful people.** They label productive individuals as *"money-grubbers"* or *"thieves."*

5. **Excuses for financial struggles.** They attribute others' success to *"luck"* or *"connections,"* convincing themselves they are superior for having less.

6. **Condemnation of financial wisdom.** They view those who study or act on financial matters as *"shallow."*

7. **A false sense of spiritual superiority.** They believe having less money makes them more righteous or mature.

The devil distorts truth through theological extremes. Consider the following:

- **Cessationist Theology vs. Charismatic Chaos**
- **Legalism vs. Cheap Grace**
- **Hyper-Focus on God's Love vs. Hyper-Focus on God's Judgment**
- **The Prosperity Gospel vs. The Pride of Poverty**

A spirit of poverty warps thinking, leading believers to say things like:*"I don't need (or want) more money."* And/or: *"I just want enough to get by."*

This is often an attempt to appear humble, content, or spiritual. However, this mindset does not stem from humility—it stems from a spirit of poverty and spiritual pride.

Ironically, such thinking is selfish.

Why?

Because who knows how many people you could bless if you increased your income significantly?

The Bible is clear: God doesn't want you to just get by—He wants you to create wealth (Deuteronomy 8:18). That's why He gave you the ability to do so.

However, many believers mistakenly equate wealth with extreme examples—imagining they must become a Wall Street tycoon, a real estate mogul, or a billionaire investor.

Nothing could be further from reality.

Your ability to create wealth is directly tied to:

- *Your resourcefulness*
- *Your creativity*
- *Your boldness for the King*
- *Your management of what you already have*
- *Your willingness to take risks*
- *Your relationships*
- *Your natural talents and spiritual gifts*
- *Your confidence in the Kingdom's abundance*
- *Your willingness to forsake all to follow Him*

These are the tools God gives us to create wealth. No one can claim they have *no* faith, *no* resourcefulness, *no* creativity, or *no* relationships. We all have something valuable to work with.

Remember the Parable of the Talents?

God gave each servant *according to their ability*. He has given each of us a measure of faith, spiritual gifts, and talents. He has equipped us for success—and, most importantly, He has given us His Holy Spirit!

The Final Question

So now, the question remains:

What will YOU do with what God has given you?

Yes, dear friend, the choice is yours. The purpose of this book was to stir you into bold action for the Kingdom of God.

My goal was to correct any perverse thinking you may have unknowingly adopted concerning money and prosperity. These false beliefs not only affect financial well-being but also impact marriages, family life, and perceptions of God. They keep believers defeated and bound—but truth sets us *free*.

If you've read this far with an open heart and mind, I commend you.

If you, like I once did, believed that money, success, ambition, and prosperity were *inherently* wrong, I hope this book has opened your eyes. I pray it helps you reconsider your views on wealth, personal growth, and success.

My life changed when I embraced God's perspective on prosperity. I know yours can too.

Above all, I pray this book has freed you from negative beliefs about wealth, success, and—most importantly—about God.

Like the apostle John, I declare over you:

"Beloved, I pray that you may prosper in all things and be in health, just as your soul prospers." ~3 John 2, NKJV

APPENDIX
Prosperity Scriptures

A compilation from the authorized version (KJV)

Throughout the Bible, God consistently reminds us that He will prosper those who obey and love Him. In this appendix, I have compiled some of the most prominent Scriptures on prosperity. These words from your Father will reassure you that His will is for your prosperity. Read them aloud regularly to grow in faith, align your mindset with His, and experience prosperity.

Always remember, for us, these Scriptures stand as promises from God; but for Him, they stand as prophecies. His promises are always 'YES' and 'AMEN.' His Word will always accomplish His purpose. As He said Himself:

"For as the rain comes down, and the snow from heaven, and does not return there, but waters the earth, making it bring forth and bud, that it may give seed to the sower, and bread to the eater: so shall My word be that goes forth from My mouth; it shall not return to Me void, but it shall accomplish

what I please, and it shall prosper in the thing for which I sent it." ~Isaiah 55:10-11

If you have been struggling financially, or if you're finding it difficult to grasp the teachings in this book (such as the idea that God wants you to prosper), or if you've fallen victim to a spirit of poverty, you will want to read these Scriptures every day to reclaim your freedom.

Reading God's Word on prosperity will work in your heart and mind, cultivating right belief concerning your finances. For even greater results in building your faith, read the Scriptures aloud. As Romans 10:17 reminds us, *"faith comes by hearing, and hearing by the word of God"* (NKJV).

Remember, we actually 'hear' the words that proceed from our own mouths. And when these words are God's words, it shall be well with us.

I firmly believe in the scriptural promise God gave to Joshua in Joshua 1:8:

"This Book of the Law shall not depart from your mouth, but you shall meditate in it day and night, that you may observe to do according to all that is written in it; for then you will make your way prosperous, and then you will have good success" (Emphasis mine).

It is my prayer and hope that you will be refreshed and financially blessed as you read and meditate on these Scriptures daily.

Old Testament

"And Abram was very rich in cattle, in silver, and in gold." ~Genesis 13:2

"And Lot also, which went with Abram, had flocks, and herds, and tents. And the land was not able to bear them, that they might dwell together: for their substance was great, so that they could not dwell together." ~Genesis 13:5-6

"And the Lord said unto Abram, after that Lot was separated from him, Lift up now thine eyes, and look from the place where thou art northward, and southward, and eastward, and westward: For all the land which thou seest, to thee will I give it, and to thy seed for ever. And I will make thy seed as the dust of the earth: so that if a man can number the dust of the earth, then shall thy seed also be numbered. Arise, walk through the land in the length of it and in the breadth of it; for I will give it unto thee." ~Genesis 13:14-17

"And when Abram was ninety years old and nine, the Lord appeared to Abram, and said unto him, I am the

Almighty God; walk before me, and be thou perfect. And I will make my covenant between me and thee, and will multiply thee exceedingly. And Abram fell on his face: and God talked with him, saying, As for me, behold, my covenant is with thee, and thou shalt be a father of many nations. Neither shall thy name any more be called Abram, but thy name shall be Abraham; for a father of many nations have I made thee. And I will make thee exceeding fruitful, and I will make nations of thee, and kings shall come out of thee. And I will establish my covenant between me and thee and thy seed after thee in their generations for an everlasting covenant, to be a God unto thee, and to thy seed after thee. And I will give unto thee, and to thy seed after thee, the land wherein thou art a stranger, all the land of Canaan, for an everlasting possession; and I will be their God. And God said unto Abraham, thou shalt keep my covenant therefore, thou, and thy seed after thee in their generations." ~Genesis 17:1-9

"Then Isaac sowed in that land, and received in the same year an hundredfold: and the Lord blessed him. And the man waxed great, and went forward, and grew until he became very great: For he had possession of flocks, and possession of herds, and great store of servants: and the Philistines envied him." ~Genesis 26:12-14

"But the Lord was with Joseph, and shewed him mercy, and gave him favour in the sight of the keeper of the prison. And the keeper of the prison committed to Joseph's hand all the prisoners that were in the prison; and whatsoever they did there, he was the doer of it. The keeper of the prison looked not to any thing that was under his hand; because the Lord was with him, and that which he did, the Lord made it to prosper." ~Genesis 39:21-23

"If ye walk in my statutes, and keep my commandments, and do them; Then I will give you rain in due season, and the land shall yield her increase, and the trees of the field shall yield their fruit. And your threshing shall reach unto the vintage, and the vintage shall reach unto the sowing time: and ye shall eat your bread to the full, and dwell in your land safely." ~Leviticus 26:3-5

"For the Lord thy God hath blessed thee in all the works of thy hand: he knoweth thy walking through this great wilderness: these forty years the Lord thy God hath been with thee; thou hast lacked nothing." ~Deuteronomy 2:7

"But the land, whither ye go to possess it, is a land of hills and valleys, and drinketh water of the rain of heaven: A land which the Lord thy God careth for: the eyes of the Lord thy God are always upon it, from

the beginning of the year even unto the end of the year. And it shall come to pass, if ye shall hearken diligently unto my commandments which I command you this day, to love the Lord your God, and to serve him with all your heart and with all your soul, That I will give you the rain of your land in his due season, the first rain and the latter rain, that thou mayest gather in thy corn, and thy wine, and thine oil. And I will send grass in thy fields for thy cattle, that thou mayest eat and be full."
~Deuteronomy 11:11-15

"And it shall come to pass, if thou shalt hearken diligently unto the voice of the Lord thy God, to observe and to do all his commandments which I command thee this day, that the Lord thy God will set thee on high above all nations of the earth: And all these blessings shall come on thee, and overtake thee, if thou shalt hearken unto the voice of the Lord thy God. Blessed shalt thou be in the city, and blessed shalt thou be in the field. Blessed shall be the fruit of thy body, and the fruit of thy ground, and the fruit of thy cattle, the increase of thy kine, and the flocks of thy sheep. Blessed shall be thy basket and thy store. Blessed shalt thou be when thou comest in, and blessed shalt thou be when thou goest out. The Lord shall cause thine enemies that rise up against thee to be smitten before thy face: they shall come out against thee one way, and flee before thee seven

ways. The Lord shall command the blessing upon thee in thy storehouses, and in all that thou settest thine hand unto; and he shall bless thee in the land which the Lord thy God giveth thee. The Lord shall establish thee an holy people unto himself, as he hath sworn unto thee, if thou shalt keep the commandments of the Lord thy God, and walk in his ways. And all people of the earth shall see that thou art called by the name of the Lord; and they shall be afraid of thee. And the Lord shall make thee plenteous in goods, in the fruit of thy body, and in the fruit of thy cattle, and in the fruit of thy ground, in the land which the Lord sware unto thy fathers to give thee. The Lord shall open unto thee his good treasure, the heaven to give the rain unto thy land in his season, and to bless all the work of thine hand: and thou shalt lend unto many nations, and thou shalt not borrow. And the Lord shall make thee the head, and not the tail; and thou shalt be above only, and thou shalt not be beneath; if that thou hearken unto the commandments of the Lord thy God, which I command thee this day, to observe and to do them."
~Deuteronomy 28:1-13

"See, I have set before thee this day life and good, and death and evil; In that I command thee this day to love the Lord thy God, to walk in his ways, and to keep his commandments and his statutes and his judgments, that thou mayest live and multiply: and the Lord thy God shall bless thee in the land whither thou goest to possess it." ~Deuteronomy 30:15-16

"I call heaven and earth to record this day against you, that I have set before you life and death, blessing and cursing: therefore choose life, that both thou and thy seed may live: That thou mayest love the Lord thy God, and that thou mayest obey his voice, and that thou mayest cleave unto him: for he is thy life, and the length of thy days: that thou mayest dwell in the land which the Lord sware unto thy fathers, to Abraham, to Isaac, and to Jacob, to give them." ~Deuteronomy 30:19-20

"This book of the law shall not depart out of thy mouth; but thou shalt meditate therein day and night, that thou mayest observe to do according to all that is written therein: for then thou shalt make thy way prosperous, and then thou shalt have good success." ~Joshua 1:8

"And keep the charge of the Lord thy God, to walk in his ways, to keep his statutes, and his commandments, and his judgments, and his testimonies, as it is written in the law of Moses, that thou mayest prosper in all that thou doest, and whithersoever thou turnest thyself." ~1 Kings 2:3

"Then shalt thou prosper, if thou takest heed to fulfil the statutes and judgments which the Lord charged

Moses with concerning Israel: be strong, and of good courage; dread not, nor be dismayed." ~1 Chronicles 22:13

"Thine, O Lord is the greatness, and the power, and the glory, and the victory, and the majesty: for all that is in the heaven and in the earth is thine; thine is the kingdom, O Lord, and thou art exalted as head above all. Both riches and honour come of thee, and thou reignest over all; and in thine hand is power and might; and in thine hand it is to make great, and to give strength unto all." ~1 Chronicles 29:11-12

"And they rose early in the morning, and went forth into the wilderness of Tekoa: and as they went forth, Jehoshaphat stood and said, Hear me, O Judah, and ye inhabitants of Jerusalem; Believe in the Lord your God, so shall ye be established; believe his prophets, so shall ye prosper." ~2 Chronicles 20:20

"And he sought God in the days of Zechariah, who had understanding in the visions of God: and as long as he sought the Lord, God made him to prosper." ~2 Chronicles 26:5

"And in every work that he began in the service of the house of God, and in the law, and in the commandments, to seek his God, he did it with all his heart, and prospered." ~2 Chronicles 31:21

"If they obey and serve him, they shall spend their days in prosperity, and their years in pleasures." ~Job 36:11

"Blessed is the man that walketh not in the counsel of the ungodly, nor standeth in the way of sinners, nor sitteth in the seat of the scornful. But his delight is in the law of the Lord; and in his law doth he meditate day and night. And he shall be like a tree planted by the rivers of water, that bringeth forth his fruit in his season; his leaf also shall not wither; and whatsoever he doeth shall prosper." ~Psalm 1:1-3

"The Lord is my shepherd; I shall not want." ~Psalm 23:1

"The young lions do lack, and suffer hunger: but they that seek the Lord shall not want any good thing." ~Psalm 34:10

"Let the Lord be magnified, which hath pleasure in the prosperity of his servant." ~Psalm 35:27

"Trust in the Lord, and do good; so shalt thou dwell in the land, and verily thou shalt be fed. Delight thyself also in the Lord: and he shall give thee the desires of thine heart. Commit thy way unto the Lord; trust also in him; and he shall bring it to pass. And he shall bring forth thy righteousness as the light, and thy judgment as the noonday. Rest in the

Lord, and wait patiently for him: fret not thyself because of him who prospereth in his way, because of the man who bringeth wicked devices to pass." ~Psalm 37:3-7

"I have been young, and now am old; yet have I not seen the righteous forsaken, nor his seed begging bread." ~Psalm 37:25

"Blessed be the Lord, who daily loadeth us with benefits, even the God of our salvation." ~Psalm 68:19

"For the Lord God is a sun and shield: the Lord will give grace and glory: no good thing will he withhold from them that walk uprightly." ~Psalm 84:11

"The righteous shall flourish like the palm tree: he shall grow like a cedar in Lebanon. Those that be planted in the house of the Lord shall flourish in the courts of our God. They shall still bring forth fruit in old age; they shall be fat and flourishing; to shew that the Lord is upright: he is my rock, and there is no unrighteousness in him." ~Psalm 92:12-15

"Praise ye the Lord. Blessed is the man that feareth the Lord, that delighteth greatly in his commandments. His seed shall be mighty upon earth: the generation of the upright shall be blessed.

Wealth and riches shall be in his house: and his righteousness endureth for ever." ~Psalm 112:1-3

"He will bless them that fear the Lord, both small and great. The Lord shall increase you more and more, you and your children." ~Psalm 115:13-14

"Save now, I beseech thee, O Lord: O Lord, I beseech thee, send now prosperity." ~Psalm 118:25

"Pray for the peace of Jerusalem: they shall prosper that love thee. Peace be within thy walls, and prosperity within thy palaces." ~Psalm 122:6-7

"Blessed is every one that feareth the Lord; that walketh in his ways. For thou shalt eat the labour of thine hands: happy shalt thou be, and it shall be well with thee." ~Psalm 128:1-2

"If thy children will keep my covenant and my testimony that I shall teach them [...] I will abundantly bless her provision: I will satisfy her poor with bread. I will also clothe her priests with salvation: and her saints shall shout aloud for joy. There will I make the horn of David to bud: I have ordained a lamp for mine anointed. His enemies will I clothe with shame: but upon himself shall his crown flourish." ~Psalm 132:12-18

"Honour the Lord with thy substance, and with the firstfruits of all thine increase: So shall thy barns be filled with plenty, and thy presses shall burst out with new wine." ~Proverbs 3:9-10

"Riches and honour are with me; yea, durable riches and righteousness. My fruit is better than gold, yea, than fine gold; and my revenue than choice silver. I lead in the way of righteousness, in the midst of the paths of judgment: That I may cause those that love me to inherit substance; and I will fill their treasures." ~Proverbs 8:18-21

"The Lord will not suffer the soul of the righteous to famish: but he casteth away the substance of the wicked. He becometh poor that dealeth with a slack hand: but the hand of the diligent maketh rich. He that gathereth in summer is a wise son: but he that sleepeth in harvest is a son that causeth shame. Blessings are upon the head of the just: but violence covereth the mouth of the wicked." ~Proverbs 10:3-6

"The blessing of the Lord, it maketh rich, and he addeth no sorrow with it." ~Proverbs 10:22

"The desire of the righteous shall be granted." ~Proverbs 10:24

"There is that scattereth, and yet increaseth; and there is that withholdeth more than is meet, but it tendeth to poverty. The liberal soul shall be made fat: and he that watereth shall be watered also himself." ~Proverbs 11:24-25

"The soul of the sluggard desireth, and hath nothing: but the soul of the diligent shall be made fat." ~Proverbs 13:4

"A good man leaveth an inheritance to his children's children: and the wealth of the sinner is laid up for the just." ~Proverbs 13:22

"He that hath pity upon the poor lendeth unto the Lord; and that which he hath given will he pay him again." ~Proverbs 19:17

"Through wisdom is an house builded; and by understanding it is established: And by knowledge shall the chambers be filled with all precious and pleasant riches." ~Proverbs 24:3-4

"He that giveth unto the poor shall not lack: but he that hideth his eyes shall have many a curse." ~Proverbs 28:27

"Every man also to whom God hath given riches and wealth, and hath given him power to eat thereof, and to take his portion, and to rejoice in his labour; this is the gift of God." ~Ecclesiastes 5:19

"A feast is made for laughter, and wine maketh merry: but money answereth all things." ~Ecclesiastes 10:19

"If ye be willing and obedient, ye shall eat the good of the land." ~Isaiah 1:19

"And if thou draw out thy soul to the hungry, and satisfy the afflicted soul; then shall thy light rise in obscurity, and thy darkness be as the noon day: And the Lord shall guide thee continually, and satisfy thy soul in drought, and make fat thy bones: and thou shalt be like a watered garden, and like a spring of water, whose waters fail not." ~Isaiah 58:10-11

"Blessed is the man that trusteth in the Lord, and whose hope the Lord is. For he shall be as a tree planted by the waters, and that spreadeth out her roots by the river, and shall not see when heat cometh, but her leaf shall be green; and shall not be careful in the year of drought, neither shall cease from yielding fruit." ~Jeremiah 17:7-8

"For I know the thoughts that I think toward you, saith the Lord, thoughts of peace, and not of evil, to give you an expected end." ~Jeremiah 29:11

"Bring ye all the tithes into the storehouse, that there may be meat in mine house, and prove me now herewith, saith the Lord of hosts, if I will not open you the windows of heaven, and pour you out a blessing, that there shall not be room enough to receive it. And I will rebuke the devourer for your sakes, and he shall not destroy the fruits of your ground; neither shall your vine cast her fruit before the time in the field, saith the Lord of hosts. And all nations shall call you blessed: for ye shall be a delightsome land, saith the Lord of hosts." ~Malachi 3:10-12

New Testament

"Therefore take no thought, saying, What shall we eat? or, What shall we drink? or, Wherewithal shall we be clothed? (For after all these things do the Gentiles seek:) for your heavenly Father knoweth that ye have need of all these things. But seek ye first the kingdom of God, and his righteousness; and all these things shall be added unto you." ~Matthew 6:31-33

"And Jesus answered and said, Verily I say unto you, There is no man that hath left house, or brethren, or sisters, or father, or mother, or wife, or children, or lands, for my sake, and the gospel's, But he shall receive an hundredfold now in this time, houses, and brethren, and sisters, and mothers, and children, and lands, with persecutions; and in the world to come eternal life." ~Mark 10:29-30

"Give, and it shall be given unto you; good measure, pressed down, and shaken together, and running over, shall men give into your bosom. For with the same measure that ye mete withal it shall be measured to you again." ~Luke 6:38

"Fear not, little flock; for it is your Father's good pleasure to give you the kingdom." ~Luke 12:32

"Nevertheless he left not himself without witness, in that he did good, and gave us rain from heaven, and fruitful seasons, filling our hearts with food and gladness." ~Acts 14:17

"He that spared not his own Son, but delivered him up for us all, how shall he not with him also freely give us all things?" ~Romans 8:32

"He which soweth sparingly shall reap also sparingly; and he which soweth bountifully shall reap also bountifully. Every man according as he purposeth in his heart, so let him give; not grudgingly, or of necessity: for God loveth a cheerful giver. And God is able to make all grace abound toward you; that ye, always having all sufficiency in all things, may abound to every good work" ~2 Corinthians 9:6-8

"Now unto him that is able to do exceeding abundantly above all that we ask or think, according to the power that worketh in us." ~Ephesians 3:20

"But my God shall supply all your need according to his riches in glory by Christ Jesus." ~Philippians 4:19

"But without faith it is impossible to please him: for he that cometh to God must believe that he is, and that he is a rewarder of them that diligently seek him." ~Hebrews 11:6

"Every good gift and every perfect gift is from above, and cometh down from the Father of lights, with whom is no variableness, neither shadow of turning." ~James 1:17

"His divine power hath given unto us all things that pertain unto life and godliness, through the knowledge of him that hath called us to glory and virtue." ~2 Peter 1:3

"Beloved, I wish above all things that thou mayest prosper and be in health, even as thy soul prospereth." ~3 John 2

"And from Jesus Christ, who is the faithful witness, and the first begotten of the dead, and the prince of the kings of the earth. Unto him that loved us, and washed us from our sins in his own blood, And hath made us kings and priests unto God and his Father; to him be glory and dominion for ever and ever."
~Revelation 1:5-6

ABOUT THE AUTHOR

Sebastien Richard is a bilingual leadership expert, seasoned Bible teacher, and thought leader. Born in Montreal, he now resides in Prince Edward Island, Canada, where he leads a simple life—writing and publishing impactful books, corralling three kids, and discussing Bigfoot theories over pizza and family movie nights. Along with his beloved wife, Elisabeth, he founded *Thriving on Purpose Ministries*.

Raised in the humbler quarters of Montreal by a family richer in love than money, Sebastien found his true calling through the words of the Bible, his relationship with Jesus Christ, and his passion for writing and researching the Scriptures, the controversial, and the mysterious. With Elisabeth, his partner in both life and ministry, he embarked on a growth journey that includes publishing under his real name (and a not-so-secret pen name).

Sebastien's goal is to explore, ponder, discover, inspire, and transform his readers, whether through dissecting ancient texts or exploring new angles on leadership and faith. His books offer a ticket to personal development, enlightenment, and a healthy dose of hard truths. Sebastien is a bona fide Renaissance man, blending deep insights with a resilient and curious mind. His teaching style combines wisdom, approachable charm, and a knack for making complex theological concepts as relatable as your favorite sitcom.

When he's not enjoying family time or sharing his biblical wisdom through his mighty pen, you can find him shouting at the TV during NHL games (go Avs go!) or chasing the truth about the latest fringe theory. As a writer, Sebastien's mission is to craft a legacy as impactful, genuine, and intriguing as the faith and enigmas he cherishes.

You can connect with Sebastien through his platforms of choice on Facebook, YouTube, and LinkedIn.

You Might Also Like These Books by SEBASTIEN RICHARD:

Just Decrees
For Your Finances:

Break Off the Spirit of Poverty
& Unlock Your Financial Breakthrough

The Devil Wants You Bound by Debt, Broke, and Financially Fruitless. So... What Are You Going to Do About It?

You are going to *decree your way to financial breakthrough, that's what!*

In **Just Decree for Your Finances** ©, author Sebastien Richard invites you to take back what the Enemy has stolen by decreeing a holy storm of heavenly financial favor.

Yes, it's time for you to start receiving wealth from the vaults of Heaven by aligning yourself with the *Word of God* in financial matters. Why? Because you've got better things to do than be in lack.

With close to two-thousand wealth-related Scriptures, the Bible is permeated with lessons and promises about finances, provision, and prosperity.

This one-of-a-kind decree compilation provides you with:

- **Breakthrough Proclamations** to bring about open heavens
- **Wisdom-Infused Decrees** to exercise godly stewardship
- **Affluence Affirmations** to speak forth financial blessing

Just Decrees for Your Finances is based on an extensive selection of money-related Scripture passages. This decree book will serve as a catalyst for your financial breakthrough and transformation for the glory of God and His Kingdom.

AVAILABLE ON:

amazon.com

KINGDOM FUNDAMENTALS

What does the Kingdom of God mean?
What does it mean for you?

How Much of The Kingdom of God Are YOU Experiencing? A Bit? Some? Not Enough?

Many believers lead lives of unavowed defeat, quiet desperation, and long for more in their lives and walk with God. The *victory,* *fire,* *living waters,* and *abundant life* they were promised, somehow elude them.

Has Christianity failed them? Has the Church dropped the ball? Is there something more? Something... *better?* The answer to all these questions is an emphatic *yes!*

The Kingdom of God was the central theme of Jesus' teachings. And yet, it has been (and still is) one of the most neglected and misunderstood teachings in Church history. Just as it was in Jesus' days, many are still bound by the *'doctrines and commandments of men'* today (Mark 7:7, Matthew 15:9). The results of this Kingdom neglect, which are found in most denominations today and in the lives of their congregants, are disquieting at best.

In ***Kingdom Fundamentals***, Sebastien Richard invites you to undertake and pursue your own *'Kingdom Quest'* by dropping the shackles of religion, redefining your purpose, and rediscovering the Kingdom God *'prepared for you since the creation of the world.'*

Encounter the glory of the Kingdom afresh through new and profound revelations of its King, its power, its majesty, and most of all... *Your place and purpose in it!*

AVAILABLE ON:

amazon.com

Also from Thriving on Purpose Publishing:

The Science of Getting Rich
Enhanced Classic Edition

By Wallace D. Wattles

Unlock the secrets to financial success and personal growth with the timeless wisdom of Wallace Delois Wattles' groundbreaking classic!

The Science of Getting Rich has inspired countless individuals to achieve wealth and prosperity through the power of thought, will, and action. This enhanced edition brings you even closer to these transformative principles with added insights and practical steps for achieving your goals.

Why This Enhanced Edition?

★ **Complete, Unabridged, Original Text by Wallace D. Wattles:** Experience the full impact of Wattles' pioneering work, presented in its entirety for a comprehensive understanding of his teachings.

★ **Added Insights and Actionable Steps to Wealth:** At the end of each chapter, discover a key takeaway, an affirmation, and a call to action designed to reinforce the chapter's principles and propel you toward financial success.

★ **Enhanced and Readable 12pt Font:** Enjoy a smooth reading experience with a clear, easily readable font that makes absorbing Wattles' wisdom effortless.

This unique edition of *The Science of Getting Rich* not only preserves the original text but also amplifies its impact with practical tools for today's readers.

Whether you're a longtime follower of Wattles' teachings or new to his compelling insights, this book provides the perfect blend of ageless wisdom, actionable steps, and modern-day application. You're invited to take the first step towards your personal prosperity and unlock the divine potential of your mind.

"There is a science of getting rich, and it is an exact science, like algebra or arithmetic. There are certain laws which govern the process of acquiring riches, and once these laws are learned and obeyed by anyone, that person will get rich with mathematical certainty."

~**Wallace Delois Wattles, The Science of Getting Rich**

The Art of Money Getting

Enhanced Edition with
Key Takeaways and Modern-Day Application

By P.T. Barnum

Unlock timeless financial wisdom with this enhanced edition of P.T. Barnum's classic work on the fine art of acquiring wealth.

Known as the ultimate showman, Phineas Taylor (P.T.) Barnum's insights into financial success remain as relevant today as they were in the 19th century. This *Wealth Wisdom Classics* © edition not only includes the complete and unabridged original text, but also features end-of-chapter takeaways and modern-day applications to help you navigate today's financial landscape.

This enhanced edition features the following:

★ **Complete and Unabridged Original Text:** Experience Barnum's wisdom in its entirety.

★ **Easy-to-Read 12pt Font Throughout:** Enjoy a comfortable reading experience.

★ **Additional End-of-Chapter Takeaways and Applications:** Practical insights and actionable steps to apply Barnum's advice in today's modern world.

Whether you're an entrepreneur, a business professional, a personal growth enthusiast, or simply someone seeking to improve your financial acumen, *The Art of Money Getting* offers invaluable and ageless guidance. Learn from one of history's most successful showmen, visionaries, innovators and entrepreneurs and apply his wisdom-infused principles to achieve your own financial success.

"Money is, in some respects, like fire. It is a very excellent servant, but a terrible master." ~**P. T. Barnum, The Art of Money Getting**

ENJOYED THIS BOOK?

If so, please be kind and leave a review on: